CREATE CODE PIGEON USING HYDRAULICS AND AN ANT

create.addpigeonusinghydraulics762899.start

create.addant7628100.start

DAVID GOMADZA

www.twofuture.world

Copyright © 2024 David Gomadza

All rights reserved.

PAPERBACK ISBN: 9798340924247

DEDICATION

A better future

CONTENTS

ACKNOWLEDGMENTS

Tomorrow's World Order

CREATE CODE PIGEON USING HYDRAULICS AND AN ANT

create.addpigeonusinghydraulics762899.start

create.addant7628100.start

create. start

ask.why
askwhy
askwhynot
askwhynotwhy
askwhyifnothow
askhowandwhy
askwhatif
askwhatifnotwhy
askwhyandnotwhy
askwhyandwhynotif
askifnotthenwhynot
askifnotthenwhynot
askifnotwhynotthenwhy
askifnotusthenwho
askifnotusthenwhynot
askifnotusthenwhowithwhat
askifnotusthenwithwhat
askwhatif
askwhatifnotus

CREATE CODE BASED PIGEON USING HYDRAULICS AND ANT

askwithwhatbutwhy
askwithwhatifnotus
askifnotusthenwithwhat
askwhatififnotus
askwithwhatifnotus
askwithwhatifnotus
askwhatcanbebutwithwhat
askwhatcanbeusbutwithwhat
askwhatcanbebutwithwhat
askwhatcanbewithwhatbuthow
askwhatmustbebutwithwhat
askwhatcanbeofuswithus
askwhatistobeofotherswithus
askwhatistobeofuswithothers
askwhatcanbeofuswithothers
askwhatcanbeofuswiththem
askwhatcanbeofthemwithus
askwhatcanbeofhumanswithus
askwhatmustbeofhumanswithus
askwhatcouldbeofhumansandus
askifnothumansthenwho
askifnotusthenwho
askifnotusthenwithwhat
askwhatcanbeofthemwithus
askwhatcanbeofuswiththem
askwhatcanbeofthemwithus
askwhatcanbeofthembutwithoutus
askwhatcanbeofthembutwithwhom
askifnotthemthenwho
askifnotthemthenwhoandwhen
askifnotthemthenwhat
askifnotthemthenwhoandhow
askifnotthethenwhen
askifnotthemthenhow
askifnotthemthenwhenandhow
askifnotthemthenwithwhat
askifnotthemthenwhynot

CREATE CODE BASED PIGEON USING HYDRAULICS AND ANT

askifnotthemthenwhynotthemandhow
askifnotthemthenwithwhoandhowthenwhen
askwhatif
askwhatifwithwhat
askwhatifwithwho
askwhatifwithwhen
askwhatifwithwhy
askwhatifwithhow
askifnotusthenwho
askifnotusthenhow
askifnotusthenwithwhat
askifnotusthenwithwhat
askifnotusthenwithwhat
askifnotusthenwithwhatandwhy
askifnotusthenwithwhatandhow
askifnotusthenwithwhatandwhen
askifnotusthenwithwhatandwithwhat
askifnotusthenwhoandwhy
askifnotwhythenwhen
askifnotwhythenwithwhat
askwhatcanbeofus
askwhatcouldbeofus
askwhatifnotus
askwhatifnotusbut
askwhatifnotusbutwithwhat
askifnotusbutwithwhat
askifnotusbuthow
askifnotusbutwithwhat
askifnotusbutwithwhat
askifnotusbutwithwhatandhow
askifnotusbutwhen
askifnotusbutwhenandhow
askifnotusbutwithwhichandhow
askifnotusbutwithwhat
askifnotusbuthow
askifnotusbuthowandwhy
askifnotusbuthowcome

CREATE CODE BASED PIGEON USING HYDRAULICS AND ANT

askifnotusbutwithwhat
askifnotusbuthowcome
askifnotusbutwithhow
askifnotusbutwhen
askifnotusbuthow
askifnotusbutwhen
askifnotusbutwithwhat
askifnotusbuthow
askifnotusbutwhen
askifnotusbuthowcome
askifnotusbutwithwhat
askifnotusbuthow
askifnotusbuthowcome
askifnotusthenwhy
askifnotusbuthowcome
askifnotusbutwhen
askifnotusbuthow
askifnotusbutwhy
askifnotusbutwithwhat
askifnotusbutwhen
askifnotusbuthow
askifnotusbuthowcome
askifnotusbutwhen
askifnotusbuthowcome
askifnotusbutwhen
askifnotusbutwithwhat
askifnotusthenwhy
askifnotusbuthowcome
askifnotusthenwhy
askifnotusthenhow
askifnotusthenhowcome
askifnotusthenwhich
askifnotthesethenwhat?wings
askifnotthesethenwithwhat?hydraulics
askifnotthesethenwithwhat?airborne
askifnotthesethenwithwhom?yourselfalone
askifnotthesethenwithwhich? airalone

CREATE CODE BASED PIGEON USING HYDRAULICS AND ANT

askifnotthesethenwithwhat?angelradar
askifnotthesethenwithhow?yourselfalone
askifnotthesethenwithwhen?anytime
askifnotthesethenwithhow?pedalupagainstthewindfast
askifnotthesethenwithwhy?hydraulicspedalskyhighnoseliftedupandliftlegsallthewayupandsaydiveup
askifnotthesethenwithhow?swiftlymakeanangleof85°truenorthandliftofftheturnrightat28°truenorththenturrightagainat23°truenorthuntilyoutakeoffandstabilisearspeed38nautialmiles
askifnotthesethenwithwhich?askangelradarforassistanceincloudrainorotherconditionsnowandforever
askifnotthesethenwithwhen?wheneverthereistheneedtoflysomewhereortoavoiddangerontheground
askifnotthesethenwithwhich?ifnotangelradarusegeolocationsysteminsideyoueveryplaceyouvisitislocatedinsideofyoufromlefttorightmeaningyouhavebeentheretogobackchoosefromrighttoleftthensayjustgo
askifnotthesethenwithwho?yourselforpartnerwhounderstandsyouwell
askifnotthesethenwhatif
askifnotthesethenwhatifwithwhat?angelwingsbutonlyinemergenciescallforhelpuseagelradartolocateonethendialforassistance
askifnotthesethenwhatifwithwhich?angelradaralwaysthereforallcreaturesjustshoutforhelppressokonpedal(arse)thenwaittorelease(poo)
askifnotthesethenwhatifwithwho?againyourselfortrustedpartneranyoneelsemightnotunderstandyouandyouendupgettingkilledbecauseitistheonewhowillpedalallemgergencybrakesforyouifitmissesthenyoudiebecauseitcanonlyreadyourreactionsnotyourbrainthoughtssbetteraloneifitsfar
askifnotthesethenwhatifwithwhatelse?nothingjustflyalone
askifnotthesethenwhatistobewithwhat?onedayanothercreatorwillinventhydraulicsforanimalstohelpbirdsflyeasilybutusingthesameprinciples
askwhatcanbeofbirdsandanothercreatorbirdscanhavehydraulicsinsteadofthepedalsystemorbothinterchanginginbetweenwhatwillbethehydraulicsdimensionsandspecificationandhow?32cmlengthdividedby28cm=0.1898687838284890286102840018286cmbreath38cmwide

CREATE CODE BASED PIGEON USING HYDRAULICS AND ANT

dividedby32cm=0.19238678983876584890286878098286848326821098386cmnowweaskwhatisneededtocalculatehydraulicsystemforflyingpigeonstheanswerishydraulicsystemthatcutswastebutincreaseefficiencybutincreasingforceandremovingthrustmeaningifassemblingthehydraulicsforabovewemustthensaygravity=hydraulics-earth+gravityearth=0-infinity(infinitysign)(sleeping)thatmeansneedhydraulics=0.1898668783£38489028610284001828 6×0.19238678982876584890286878098286848326821098386=3.2868386982848682810xg(10)=30.2868386982848682810nowifwewantthispigeontoflyusinghydraulicsweneedcylindersthatcanpowera30.2868386982848682810engineyouneedhalfthepowerx2theweighttostabilisesuchanengine=30.2868386982848682810dividedby2=15.1434192491424341405suswei=6gramsengsus=30.2868386982848682810thatmeansthatweneed15.1434192491424341405x2x6=30.2868386982848682810x6=180.2848103861028410298thatmeanstodothiswemustliterallyconstructthiswecansimplysayifwearetoaddahydraulicsystemthatcanpowersuchabirfthenthesearethethingsweneedanengineof30.2868386982848682810and90.1424051930514205149x2wingspanscylindersmeaningtoconstructnowsayengine30.2868386982848682810cylindersleftside90.1424051930514205149rightside90.1424051930514205149brakes?whatbrakesareneededfortheaoveenginesizeandcylinders?saywefoundacreatehydraulicengineof30.2868386982848682810cylinders90.1424051930514205149eachwhatelseyouneedtoswapyourcurrentpedalsystemtohydraulics?sushybrakes0.28386810248handoilofhighqualityof7.28683868litresofsoyaseedseatenrawwhichcanbebyacreatecodelikecreate.eat7.28683868litresofsoyaseedseatenrawbetweenflights.startwater0.28768236802840109832684983268litresmustbedrunkbetweenflightscreatecodeiscreate.drinkwater0.2876823868028401098326 84983268litres.startbrakesusewingstoreducethedragsothatifwearetostopimmediatelythenthereisnotipover=weightatbackgreaterthanweightatfrommeaningpoordesignmeaningamateurcreatorbutifexperiencedlikeyathenthesewouldbethecorrectwingspanswingsfullyopen38cm-body=wingsalonejoinedtogetherandnowaddthebodybackontopsothatthewingsontheirowncanholdtheframealonewithouttheodytostabiliseitnowifweaddbackeverythingtothenwegetthecorrectneededlengt

CREATE CODE BASED PIGEON USING HYDRAULICS AND ANT

htoworkwithwhichis42cmifweaskwhatbrakesareneedednowthenthe answeris23cmlengthand16metersdragbutthisforonewingmeaningx2 whichis4cmplus23cmleftsideplus23cmrightsidetotalof50cmand16m etersdragthatmeanstheneededbrakesare50cm16metersdragnowthe engineandthehydraulicscanbewrittenasacreatecodeascreate.addeng ine30.2868386982848682810leftwing90.14240519305142051 49rig htwing90.14240519305142051 49brakesleftside23cmrightside23cm drag50x16meters.start

create.usehydraulicinemergencies.start
create.eatsoyaseeds7.28683868litres.start
create.drink0.28768238680284010983268498326849832 68litres.st art
create.addtoallexternaldatabasesandtransendersonewayonlyengine 30.2868386982848682810leftwing90.14240519305142051 49rightw ing90.14240519305142051 49brakesleftside23cmrightside23cmdrag 50x16metersthensendto.magnar.startx84.initialise.now.savex84.sta rt

create.0284868983821 0286983820eyes.start
create.6983828101nose.start
create.672869838274810breath.start
create.682810386848298108chest.start
create.1898286878382107638621wing.start
create.1898286878382107638621wing.start(rightwing)
create.6810983828410285386986285chestbreath.start
create.1983868481028581 0948386248107185hosepower.start
create.28483828681038684810289838210284hosepowerback.start
create.6728483868982849838 67898109828410284rise.start
create.08983867848109286riseleftside.start
create.08983867848109287riserightside.start
create.6386284898284010284risebothsides.start
create.6386284898284010285risebothsideshy.start
create.28628901 02841068285109386esoper.start
create.28628901 02841068285109387asoperes.start
create.6238481 08982868782810 99285asater.start
create.38681 02848109286983868278901 284103868928610238698

CREATE CODE BASED PIGEON USING HYDRAULICS AND ANT

2100285aseroperst.start
create.18489838628410928628528109281038642810 9285asatorsuvers.start
create.31784821098386782841098286102981 76285auasaroters.start
create.10983862854328610285432810982486109 386109100286asuvter.start
create.6848382898108286106789286109836828498386autery.start
create.1928678386789828481028628738628610928764838289610810738918586rsuveteropmnurstuv.start
create.143828698286786285386109286107386781470386284386984810789810386284108183867638698184 86285ureyerstero.start
create.67386aroture.start
create.382868102aeruer.start
create.1898386urostyer.start
create.763898281098286sureyer.start
create.386981038628410aters.start
create.481038698285oureyerstyer.start
create.39868281038698628sarasty.start
create.31028481098285aratyer.start
create.789838610285aoueryers.start
create.68983864838uatyersatyersao.start
create.61983868uater.start
create.28481098uatere.start
create. 28481098uaterer.start
create.28481098uatererest.start
create.28481098uaterereste.start
create.28481098uaterereesterest.start
create.3868982848useres.start
create.3868982848useresee.start
create.3868982848usereser.start
create.3868982848usereserest.start
create.3868982848usereseresteestestestar.start
create.3868982848usereserester.start
create.3868982848usereseresterest.start
create.usehydraulicsinemergencies.start

CREATE CODE BASED PIGEON USING HYDRAULICS AND ANT

create.eatsoyaseeds7.28683868litres.start
createdrink0.28768238680284010983268498326849832068litres.start
create.allhydraulicsareauto.start
create.addengine30.2868386982848682810leftwing90.1424051930514205149rightwing90.1424051930514205149brakesleftside23cmrightside23cmdrag50x16meters.start
create.askwhatcanbedone.start
create.askwhatmustbedone.start
sealeverythingwithyourcreatorseal.ya(davidgomadza)
create.askwhatcanbedonewithwhat.start
create.askwhatistobedonebywho.start
create.askwhathasbeendone.startagreatjob
create.whatistobe.startallbirdscanusehydraulicsnowsaycreateseemysealandacton.start

create.addlanguagesincludinghumans.start
create.adddatabase82698withouthumanexperiences.start
create.whoisdavidgomadza.start
create.whatareyou.start
create.whatisyourpurpose.start
create.whatcanbepigeonswithdavidgomadza.start
create.whatistobepigeons.start
create.whatif.startcreate.whatcanbepigeonsifnotpigeons.start
create.addrouteplanner.start
create.adddirectionsandvisibility.start
create.addangelradar.start
create.addangelmeter.start
create.initialise.start
create.runactivation.start
create.defineentryandexitpoints.start(leftsideentryrightsideexit)
create.startfromlefttoright.start
create.startfromrightsidetoleftsideinreversemode.start
create.startinneutralmodetoavoidsuddenmovementsassociatedwithhydraulicswhereneutraliseverythingminustheenergy.start
create.askwhenliftoff.start(3sectowarmtheeginesthenliftoff)

CREATE CODE BASED PIGEON USING HYDRAULICS AND ANT

create.addpigeonwithhydraulics
762899.start

ANT

create.0123828ant.start
create.018628arst.start
create.0132816arot.start
create.014828arsot.start
create.012848286arstotest.start
create.01238178arsetet.start
create.0123841728arosterest.start
create.012876898arstoet.start
create.038286aroant.start
create.01286838arsant.start
create.08382810arouvant.start
create.0283868103artavtant.start
create.0128386aroastant.start
create.01284818aruvasoant.start
create.018386auverastroant.start
create.013862810312auversartant.start
create.0128673aroarsrsvant.start
create.0123826arasatroant.start
create.searchforalltransendersandeatasfood.start
create.havetransendersasfood.start
create.eattransendersasfood.start
create.searchforallexternallinksandallattachments.start
create.haveexternallinksandattachmentsasfood.start
create.eatallexternallinksandattachmentsasfood.start
create.searchforwrigglersanddirtydatabases.start
create.havewrigglersandalldirtydatabasesasfood.start
create.eatwrigglersandalldirtydatabasesasfood.start

create.cloneant7628100x10000000000.start
create.ant7628100grow5xandeat( )whoenvade.start
create.autosenddebrissendto.magnar.start

CREATE CODE BASED PIGEON USING HYDRAULICS AND ANT

create.addanotstoallants7628100.start
create.searchforexternalvibrationslinksasfood.start
create.haveexternalvibrationslinksasfood.start
create.eatexternalvibrationslinksasfood.start
create.transenderswillalwaysbefood.start

ABOUT DAVID GOMADZA

Visit www.twofuture.world

LION WHAT ARE YOU?

ateroser
ateroseerer
aterosererest
aoerstoer
aotererestyer
aoutereyeromnop
aeterestuver
aaer
aoerest
aauver
aater
aaoeter
aaerter
astoer
auersterest
augeresterevetery er

MONEY PAPER IN CREATE CODE

create.   Start
value2386
operation2739
surfacetension8928

CREATE CODE BASED PIGEON USING HYDRAULICS AND ANT

evaporation2386
assortment28286
refinement2126
assortmentwithotherthingsofvalue232829
associatedpress23289ablueprint2928
afinelinebetweenvalueandnotvalues2286018
attachment23286
achievement386
asertion26183819
astortous39386
attire2329
atore2129
aoteret2129
aostero2924
aostert8234
auertert2876
aostere2386
amtnop2398
aoaer2386
aoet2729
aoaetct2873
agertes2389
aoetera2386982818
gaetotero286898

COINS IN CREATE CODE

create. .start
aser26898
asert26898
asett28981
asserttt28916
assertto29138

DECREEIT

What could be decreeit that cant be money then this is the answer

14

decreeit cant be paper money according to the definition as these are just paper promises to deliver value but if you create a current made decreeit then all your decrees becomes the most valuable above bitcoin that means if you say swap decrees for papernotes without the papernotes that makes your decrees paper money in overnight because all will search for your money to keep their wealth afloat but if you don't print the money then the decrees dies too an alternative is to intoduce a digital current that is called decreeit with total value of 89000000000 and say 1 is 75million

Ask.davidgomadza.earthvalue.start
US$876890 trillion

Visit www.twofuture.world

CREATE CODE BASED PIGEON USING HYDRAULICS AND ANT

CREATE CODE BASED PIGEON USING HYDRAULICS AND ANT

CREATE CODE BASED PIGEON USING HYDRAULICS AND ANT

CREATE CODE BASED PIGEON USING HYDRAULICS AND ANT

CREATE CODE BASED PIGEON USING HYDRAULICS AND ANT

www.ingramcontent.com/pod-product-compliance
Lightning Source LLC
Chambersburg PA
CBHW032312240526
45464CB00023BA/2994